Women, Adjust Your Jockstrap

The Uncensored Playbook to Win at Work and in Life

Also by Ellen Castro, MBA, MEd
Globally Recognized Executive Coach

Books

Spirited Leadership: 52 Ways to Build Trust

Happy in Spite of People

Journals

The Power of You

Celebrate You

Women, **Adjust Your Jockstrap**

The Uncensored Playbook to Win at Work and in Life

Ellen Castro
Chief Energizing Officer

ISBN: 0-9863499-4-1
ISBN 13: 978-0-9863499-4-2

Cataloging-in-Publication Data is on file at the Library of Congress
Igniting Works, Dallas, TX, USA

First paperback edition February 2021.

Edited by Roxann Garcia
Layout by Dawn Pelton
Photograph by ISP Studios

To all the courageous women who have changed the game.

To YOU for the courage and conviction to level the playing field.

We are stronger and more resilient than we know.

PREFACE

Reality: Women do have more challenges in the workplace. Do yourself a favor, get over it. Is it fair? No! Is it right? No! Is it changing? Much too slowly. Salary parity between men and women remains elusive. Wages and salaries were to be aligned in 2036. The current projection is 2056. Do you think that is realistic? Probably not, it is what it is.

Yes, there still remain invisible barriers and deeply ingrained social, cultural, religious and family conditioning and labeling regarding males and females. Double standards for the most part are alive and well in the business world. Strong men are perceived as powerful, intoxicating. Strong women are frequently perceived as bitchy, intimidating. What the heck?!

Women, the good news: *You are stronger and more resilient than you know.* You can win the game at work and in life – be a badass with a smile – by adjusting your jockstrap. This book is the uncensored playbook for breaking through invisible barriers to success, including the ones in your own mind. Thought patterns can be changed.

Imagine a life where you control
your response to fear
instead of fear controlling you.

Imagine a life where you feel
vital and invincible.

YOU have the power!

Breathe these game-changing thoughts in, feel yourself expanding through the fear into your authentic, vibrant self. *You so have this.* Change your thoughts, change your world, change the game.

Adjust Your Jockstrap is about adjusting your perspective. The game is not personal even if it feels personal. I know about taking it personally as a Latina trailblazer at good ol' boy Exxon in the 1970-1980s. Even after the 6 promotions, being a punching bag left me feeling bruised and battered with no hope. In 1985, I found myself on suicide watch in a psycho ward. Instead of shattering the glass ceiling, the glass ceiling shattered me. That demoralizing defeat is one of the best things that has happened to me. It led me to attending Harvard at age 36 to receive a second Master's Degree. The course work and counseling revealed epiphanies that led me to taking my life off autopilot, to unpacking my limiting beliefs and to begin letting go of the pattern of giving myself and my spirit away a piece at a time. And finally, to taking off my boxing gloves as a self-empowered woman – happy, comfortable and confident in any boardroom or situation.

Ducking the punch is far more productive and far less exhausting than proving you can take a punch. My mess at Exxon became my miracle. It led me to you.

You have what it takes to be a Champion
if you are willing to do the
hard work to change.

You have the power to change anything
you don't like or want.

Do you have the willingness and self-determination to do the hard work required? Are you ready to be 100% accountable for your choices, your life and your success? If you are ready, this coaching book will turn your curve balls into strength training to up your game, increase your buff-ness and multiply exponentially the likelihood for more success. This playbook of pragmatic Practices leveled the playing for me and for the countless others I have had the privilege to coach over the decades.

Reading one or more of these Practices a day can energize, uplift and unleash your potential to score big with self-awareness and self-understanding that sparks new choices and actions to thrive, not merely endure the workplace or life. I will show you how to realize a life beyond what you believe is possible today. Better choices plus better results equal more self-confidence – to exude executive presence.

To gain maximum strength for the game, make *Adjust Your Jockstrap* yours by taking "Time Outs." Write about your dreams and goals, celebrate your successes to date - which includes getting back up when it was really hard. Jot down your discoveries, insights and "ah-ha's." Consider writing affirmations that make your heart sing or that calm the raging storm in your mind. Two of my favorites are: "I am fit, fabulous and favored." and "There are no wasted experiences. Everything happens *for* me." Or perhaps use the space to doodle and draw. Drawing my smiling happy heart emitting sun rays always makes my day go better.

Reality: **No one can up your game or save you but YOU.** Your choices matter. You define you by each and every choice. Anything is possible with faith, consistency and better choices. You have what it takes. You have an inner coach that knows what is good for you and you've got me on your team cheering you on. *Your* success is personal to me.

Now is your moment. This is your time to be the Champion you are meant to be. Let the logo that anchors each Practice anchor in your heart: "I AM a Champion." Smile, adjust your jockstrap, move forward feeling supported and with hopeful expectations.

The Uncensored Playbook

YOU have the power! Be an active player in creating your amazing, winning career. Be an active player in achieving your dreams and living life fully. Self-awareness, self-reflection, self-mastery leads to self-empowerment. *You are far more powerful than you imagine.* Be your own Champion!

Accept this fact: You are already a Chief Executive Officer. You are the CEO of your brand. Your reputation precedes and proceeds you. It is always in the background. The emotional noise you create matters. Recognize your reputation is either your best PR (Public Relations) or your worst PR.

You have the life-changing powers of choice, attitude and accountability. Your every choice defines you - not your DNA, past experiences, circumstances or environment. ***YOU define you.***

No one owes you anything. Don't expect the game to change for you. You are in training. Adjust your jockstrap. You can play the game differently. You are a contender. Be the game changer. Change the game.

Take 100% ownership and accountability for your choices and be 100% committed. *Choices have consequences. Every choice counts.* Don't blame anyone for your actions. Don't allow anyone but you to decide who you are or who you will be. Have a "no excuse" mentality. *No one can save you but you.*

Meet your own needs. Stop living at the whim of others. No one's opinion of you matters more than your opinion of yourself. Do not abdicate your worth, strength or power. "What I am looking for is not out there. It is in me." Helen Keller.

Others can lend you their power; however, the power is short-lived. Lasting power comes from within. Putting your power, worth, career and happiness in the hands of others is not smart. You are definitely smarter!

There is a powerful connection between your outer experiences and your inner world. *Change your inner world, change your outer world.* As you master your thoughts and emotions *all is possible*. You are a Champion like no other. You are meant for full self-expression. *What will you show others is possible?*

Take a Time Out. Close your eyes. Imagine big. Ask yourself, "What am I here to show others is possible?" Jot down what came to you. Breathe. Smile. All is possible to those who believe and persevere.

Introspection is the breakfast for champions. Go within and sit quietly. Listen. Observe and explore your beliefs, your thoughts and your past. A belief is only a thought you keep repeating. *Don't believe everything you think.*

You have a wise inner coach that knows the truth. Don't mistake the ego as your coach. Take action on the introspection to be the world-class Champion and leader that you are.

"Experts" can be wrong. "Aerodynamically, the bumblebee shouldn't be able to fly, but the bumblebee doesn't know it, so it goes on flying anyway." Mary Kay Ash.

Proving to yourself that you can overcome a challenge builds self-esteem. Proving to others you have worth puts you at risk. Performance-based worth is fleeting. You're breathing. Worth established.

You are worthy. You deserve all the good. Feeling worthy keeps you from wandering the world for acceptance, approval and love - from people pleasing and being an approval junkie. "You had the power all along, my dear." Glenda, the Good Witch, *Wizard of Oz.*

In our society of never enough it's easy to believe we are not enough. Break the spell. Forget stigmas. ***You are enough.*** You are not an impostor. Believe in yourself. Accept what feels right for you without needing to convince others of your choice.

Follow your heart. Follow your passion. Let your heart be happy and free. Be a daydream believer. If a choice does not play out as you expected, you can choose again. "Don't stumble over something behind you." Seneca.

Only you can change the trajectory of your career and life. You can train your mind. You alone have the power over your thoughts and emotions that determine your state of strength and self-confidence. Nothing can disturb you unless you allow it.

You change the trajectory one thought, one emotion at a time. Ask yourself: "Do I feel powerful or powerless with this thought?" "Do I feel stronger or weaker with this emotion?" "Do I want this thought or emotion to create my future?" You get to choose.

Think and feel like the Champion that you are. Every time you walk by a mirror, declare, "Hello, Champion." If saying this is a stretch for you, then start with, "I'm inclined to be a Champion."

Take a Time Out. Write down 5 or more times in your life when you beamed with pride. An A on your report card? First person in the family to graduate from college? You got up when everyone thought you were down for the count? Champion Material = You.

Your self-talk – internal monologue - matters. Your subconscious is always talking and listening. Your subconscious is like the iceberg that sank the Titanic. Change your inner monologue from depleting to energizing. Winning and success begin in your mind and psyche.

Reality isn't real, it's our perception of "reality." You can change your perspective to change your reality. Your narrative impacts your experience. *What if you considered everything simply a coaching moment? What if you thought everyone was on your team for greatness – no exceptions?* You get what you expect.

If you are walking around with a chip on your shoulder for being a female, a woman of color or whatever, the expectation will create situations for the chip to be knocked off. You'll perceive a threat when none was intended. Take things curiously rather than as a threat. Seek clarification when needed.

You have no enemies, only coaches. "You may not be responsible for being down, but you must be responsible for getting up." Jesse Jackson.

The real playing field is in your mind. You have the home team advantage. You are inclined to succeed. Consider it all good, just sometimes better. Accept the fact there will be a wrestling match with old beliefs. Smile and observe. Choose the winning belief.

When your inner critic judges you harshly, call out the nonsense. Tell the critic, "That thought has no merit." Replace the non-productive, cruel inner critic with a constructive, kind possibilities coach.

It is your nature to go from success to success. Got it?! "You are your own best thing." Toni Morrison.

We have been conditioned by our culture to focus on all that is wrong instead of all that is right and good. Break the conditioning. Make a deliberate shift. Be grateful for all that is working in your life and focus only on what you want. *Put your foot on the gas.*

Make peace with your past. People and the past only have the power you give them. Pain is a clarifier. Choose to learn and grow from the pain versus dwelling and living with it. Your greatest struggles can be starting blocks. *The past does not equal your future.* With courage and compassion, it can propel you beyond your wildest imagination.

Applaud your bravery! You are courageous! Self-reflection and self-awareness are not for the weak of heart.

Start with the premise you are exactly where you need to be. If you coulda, you woulda. If you think you "should" be further along, says who? "Stop 'shoulding' all over yourself." Unknown.

The past is simply that – the past. If your story of an event is giving you a headache, choose a new narrative. Only talk about the past in a way that empowers you. *Your present thoughts create your future.* Live from your destiny, not your history.

It does not matter where you have been, it matters where you are heading. Your power to change is in this moment. Make today count. You can change. ***If you don't change, nothing changes.***

Whose life are you living – yours, someone else's or society's? Define success for you. Identify why you want it. Your definition and whys provide clarity and game smarts that help with priorities, choices and decisions. "It doesn't much matter how much you have. It all means nothing if you are not happy with yourself." Donald Duck.

Take a Time Out. Your definition of success matters. Some definitions of success can lead to illness or even death. I know. ***I was almost a statistic.*** *How will you define success?* "We must reject not only the stereotypes that others have of us but also of those that we have of ourselves." Shirley Chisholm.

Refuse to abandon yourself anymore, for any reason. *Self-respect is fundamental to living your life on your terms.* Self-respect builds strength of character, develops fortitude and provides true, authentic power.

Do you feel fulfilled and happy where you work? Is your position helping you get to where you want? Is your position maximizing your talents? If the position or environment feels stifling, choose again. There are lots of industries, companies, cultures and positions.

"Can I succeed here?" Your heart knows. Make the better decision. "Go to" something rather than "escape from" something. There are always options.

Interview for giggles. Men, in general, when applying for positions, do not ask themselves, "What if I don't meet all the qualifications?" They apply. Women tend to feel they need to have met all the requirements. Apply like a man.

Reality Check: Every day is a job interview. Answer honestly: *Would you hire you? Would you promote you?*

"Died at 30. Buried at 60." Tombstone. Discovering and living from your passion and purpose fuels your energy through the ups and downs of the economy and life. What do you care about, what are you good at and what matters most? What end result do you want? Take action today towards your end result. Smile.

Nothing is too good to be true. Nothing is impossible with faith, discipline and better choices. Keep training!

What sets your heart on fire? When do you feel most fulfilled? Spend more time, thought and energy doing these activities. Spend less time on activities that plummet your heart. As you incorporate more heart fulfilling activities into your day you are creating the life you want by reducing distractions and stressors.

Take a Time Out. Draw a heart. Write inside the heart everything that sets your heart ablaze. Outside the heart write your soul suckers. You know what to do.

Unsure of your purpose? Perhaps your purpose is being your best self. Only you can fill your niche, your way. There is no competition when you focus on being your muscular authentic self. While it is good modeling qualities you respect and admire in others, *needing* to be that person gives away your uniqueness and power.

Run your own race. You have all the credentials to be you. You are like no other. You are *that* Champion. Believe! Go the distance.

Give yourself permission to dream and achieve your boldest and happiest dreams. Find that place within you that knows nothing is impossible. *Your dreams matter.* It's never too late to change direction and achieve them – never.

Use your unique gifts, talents and qualities to the betterment of you, for the inspiration of others and service to the world. "The greatest danger for most of us is not that our aim is too high and we miss it, but that it is too low and we reach it." Michelangelo.

Drop "what ifs." Do it anyway and give it your all. We all have insecurities. We all get nervous. We all begin as novices. The worst-case scenario is you gain grit and experience. The best-case scenario you succeed! The odds are stacked in your favor. *Take a chance on you. If not you, who?*

Own your career. Own your life. Own your choices. Own the consequences. Better choices, better consequences, better results. Reality Check: *You are currently living the consequences of your past choices.*

Feeling stuck at your job because it pays well or you need the health insurance? Reframe being "stuck" to being grateful for making good money and having good benefits. Consider asking for more responsibility or interviewing for different positions. You are never stuck. Everything is a choice.

Choose to love and approve of yourself exactly as you are. Beating yourself up – our society's norm – weakens you, your strength and your game. *Be kind to you.* Acts of self-love and self-approval will help you progress more easily and quickly. "It's not your job to like me, it's mine." Byron Katie.

You are building muscle. You are toning your emotions. Smile and laugh a lot. It's all grace and growth to improve your game.

Research studies concluded that human infants are born with only 2 fears – the fear of loud noises and the fear of falling. All other fears are mind-made. Stop striking yourself out. ***What is mind-made can be changed.*** You have the power to change your thoughts. *Change your thoughts, change your world.*

Faith is having a positive expectancy about the future. Fear is having a negative expectancy. Fear is a projection of the past into the future. Don't let fear stand in your way. Smile and do it anyway. Make hope and faith your default settings to hit it out of the park!

Let life be life. Welcome change. Resistance is futile. Everything is by design. "See, I'm God. See, I lead all things to the end that I ordain for them ... by the same wisdom and love that I made them with; how should anything be amiss?" Julian of Norwich.

Take a Time Out. Is there anything you are resisting? What is the underlying fear? Is the fear true today? If the fear is real, list 3 actions you can take for a positive outcome.

Champions shift and adapt. Their motto is *"I'll give it a try."*

Begin challenging your assumptions and beliefs comprised of layers of conditioning. Stop believing anything but the truth of who you are. You are fearfully and wonderfully made. You are priceless, loved and a game changer. You are one of a kind. ***You are special.***

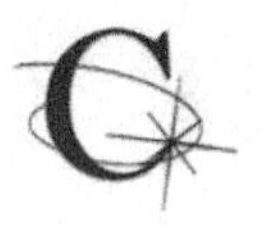

Identify your non-negotiable values. Living by your core values strengthen your character and resolve. Core values enable you to be adaptable and resilient to external factors. Compromising on your values destroys your spirit – a death by a million cuts.

Take a Time Out. If you were to live by a value, what would it be? Identify 7 specific actions that model your value. "Example is not the main thing influencing others. It is the only thing." Albert Schweitzer.

The right mental attitudes are game changers. One such attitude is "It's all a game. We win some, we 'lose' some." Stay focused and flexible. Keep smiling, dodging and playing – *never quit on you.* Take the "loss" and lesson to the next play. Be assured you will win more than you "lose."

Know that you have a reservoir of courage. Your reservoir is deeper, wider and larger than you can imagine. Use it to rise up to whatever the challenge or opportunity. You have the heart of a Champion.

Your credibility impacts your self-confidence and influences the confidence others have in you. The first question people ask themselves either consciously or subconsciously is, *"Can I trust you?"* Imagine how much simpler and more impactful your life would be if everyone trusted you.

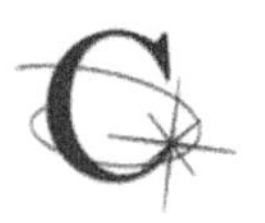

Take a Time Out. Imagine people gave you a score on how trustworthy they perceive you. Your trustworthy score ranges from 1 to 7, with 7 being high. What would be your score?

A solid reputation earns you respect and the benefit of the doubt. "A good name is worth more than riches." Solomon.

Build your credibility and power from the inside. Be conscious of your thoughts and actions. Be courageous to do the next right thing. Exhibit character and competence. Be committed to the greater good and have consistency in your actions and words as well as your moods.

People buy, help, refer and promote people they respect and like. *You earn respect and the right to be listened to regardless of your job title.* You reap what you sow. Align your intentions with your actions.

Act like a leader to be perceived as a leader. You are always on stage. "It's not overly dramatic to say your destiny hangs upon the impression you make." Barbara Walters.

Overnight sensations are a myth. There are no shortcuts to excellence. They earned their success. *Within you is everything you need to be successful and happy.* Being happy leads to better health and well-being and helps in making better decisions. Better decisions, better outcomes.

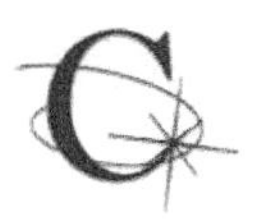

As you gain self-mastery and become more self-empowered, you will continually evaluate that which is right for you today. It's okay to change your mind. It's called maturity.

Select the good thoughts. Select the positive emotions. Select the right environment. Select the right actions. Be choosey. Choose to shine and succeed.

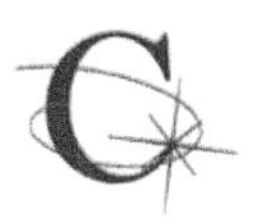

Bring your "A" game and smile even if no one is watching. A good work ethic, a spirit of excellence and a positive attitude are required regardless of your position. Make the most of what is in front of you. There is always something to learn, even if it is patience.

The company you keep impacts your brand and credibility. Seek positive relationships when growing your network of trust. Your trusted relationships are priceless assets that add points to the scoreboard.

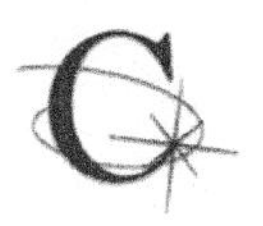

Sitting with champions is a smart play. The conversation is different. "If you are the smartest person in the room, then you are in the wrong room." Confucius.

There are no champions in the blame and shame games. You are here to live and share from your gifts, not your wounds. *You've played small long enough.* Stop all whining, grumbling and being constantly critical. It weakens you and your brand. Be solution focused. Be the attitude worth catching.

Please, never ever blame or use your time of month as an excuse. Talk about undermining your brand. No one deserves your bad or erratic moods regardless of the day or time of month.

Work and life can be much more amusing when both are considered games. "Failures" and "losing" are simply coaching moments. *We get do-overs until we master the lesson.* Isn't life grand? Once a lesson is mastered, we get another lesson. There is always more to learn if you are breathing.

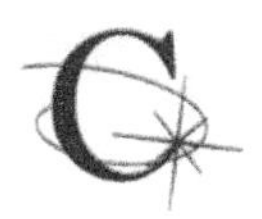

As a point of reference, you can do everything right and things can still go "wrong" – that's life. No one gets a pass. It does work out. "The way I see it, if you want the rainbow, you gotta put up with the rain." Dolly Parton.

Stay optimistic. It's quite exciting to think you have unlimited chances to begin again. Being positive is better for your stamina and health. Begin each day hoping and believing it will be a good day. Tell happy stories. Visualize your vision fulfilled. Feel the joy and excitement! They're on their way.

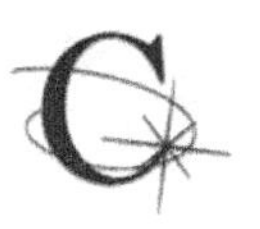

Do people seek you out for advice and counsel? Great news if the answer is yes. You've earned their respect and admiration - their trust. ***Trust is genderless.*** Trust is a noun and a verb.

Trust issues tend to be communication issues. *Everything communicates, even your silence.* Think before you speak. Be transparent. Be an effective communicator by communicating downward, upward and sideways. No one likes being blind-sided.

Communications are comprised of 7% words, 38% tone and 55% body language. What is your body language "saying?" When on the phone with someone, only 17% of the communication is words. Your tone is 83%. Let others hear your smile.

First impressions are made within 12 seconds. Make it a good one. They are hard to change. Be the first to smile. Be approachable. Invest in your wardrobe. Have good posture and a solid handshake. The web of your hand needs to connect with the web of the other person's hand. Be prepared to introduce yourself.

Take a Time Out. Develop several memorable introductions. One such introduction can be for networking events. Another one can be when you happen to ride on the elevator with a senior leader you have not met.

The majority of people judge on how fit you appear. "Fit" indicates a degree of self-discipline and pride. "Fit" is not specifically about weight. The impression revolves around appearing fit to handle what comes your way. Stay fit for you. ***You deserve your own self-care.***

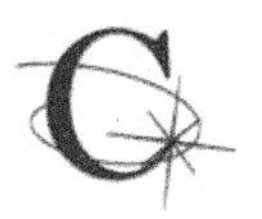

Take 3 minutes a day sitting with your eyes closed and feel love towards your body. Visualize your body getting stronger, fitter and more buff. Visualize your inner Champion expanding and getting brighter.

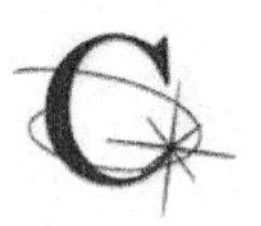

Do you stand out or blend in? Do people gravitate towards you sensing they need to meet you? Start observing the impact your presence makes to determine the level of executive presence you are exuding. People promote individuals they believe will put points on the board.

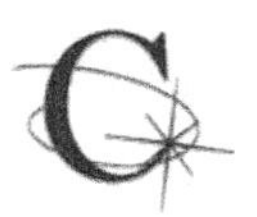

To level the playing field and succeed at work, you need to stand out in the crowd in a good way.

Men tend to take up space. Start taking up more space. It's not about your size; it's about your posture, energy and confidence. Women tend to tolerate more interruptions than men. Stop allowing interruptions. Shatter the myth that women should be seen not heard. Take back the conversation with a concise message.

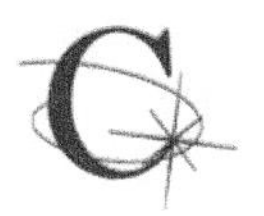

Act like you belong. Fake it till you make it. Let the Wonder Woman pose be your default - shoulders back, hands on waist with feet firmly planted on the ground. As you become Wonder Woman, stronger and confident, everyone benefits including your loved ones.

Drop the phrase "you know." The phrase can be perceived as being unsure of yourself and that you are seeking approval. Talk with authority and confidence. If you have a question, ask it. Begin noticing when and how you get in the way of your message and credibility.

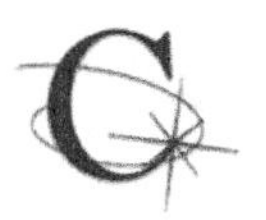

There are times to be invisible to avoid being a target. *Keeping silent when it impacts your psyche is a very different matter.*

While words are 7% of the communication, words remain critical. Choose your words carefully. If you are thinking twice about saying something, don't say it. "I've learned that people will forget what you said, forget what you did, people will never forget how you made them feel." Maya Angelou.

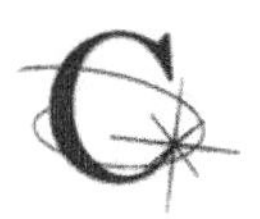

There are 3 overarching universal needs once food and shelter are supplied. The 3 universal needs are a sense of belonging, a sense of feeling appreciated and a sense of making a difference. Fulfilling those needs with each interaction makes you a Champion in the minds and hearts of individuals.

Connections of the heart are priceless. They make the impossible probable. The basics for evoking positive emotions: Be the first to smile. Make it a point to remember names, special interests and events. Be courteous. Always say "please" and "thank you." Offer encouragement and help when you can. Never hesitate to show appreciation. Keep people in the loop.

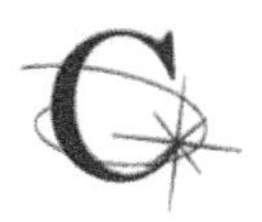

Do people feel better or worse after being in your presence? "Spread love everywhere you go. Let no one ever come to you without leaving happier." Mother Teresa.

Meaning is in people. Human behavior is context driven. The source of context can include culture, religion, education, gender, age and life experiences. The better you understand someone's frame of reference, the better equipped you are to influence, to motivate and to be heard.

Listen more than you speak. Learn to listen to understand, not to reply. Learn to listen to what is not being said. Knowledge is power.

People thrive on feedback. The intent and way you give the feedback makes *the* difference whether the message is received and acted upon. Notice the emotions you evoke when giving feedback. If the person is shutting down, ask questions instead of plowing ahead. "The delivery of the message is as important as the message itself." *Spirited Leadership.*

Giving constructive, instructive feedback is easier when you've given positive feedback in the past and you are trusted by the recipient of the feedback. *Trust is a must in business and in life.*

Caring candor takes skill and talent. Caring candor builds trust, competence, connections of the heart, followership and a winning team. When giving feedback, do people perceive you as expressing caring candor or criticizing? Reality Check: *When you turn around, is anyone there?*

People and organizations have long and at times, unforgiving memories. Under pressure do you tend to react emotionally or respond rationally? Question your emotions. Is this emotion and response appropriate for the situation?

You are changing the game! You are dispelling myths! Yes, you, mighty Champion!

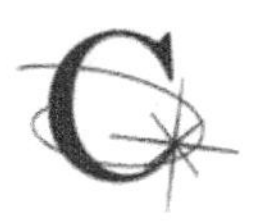

People want to be noticed, recognized and affirmed – to feel a sense of significance. Consider how your life would change for the greater if *all* your communications expressly or implicitly implied "you matter."

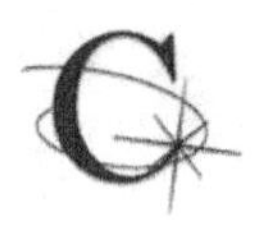

Don't waste your time attempting to change others. Spend your energy changing your reaction. You are not responsible for them. ***You are 100% responsible for you.*** Nothing can disturb you unless you allow it. "Every day brings a choice: to practice stress or to practice peace." Dr. Joan Borysenko.

Don’t believe everything you think. Question the thought, “Is this thought true today?”

Do you have a reputation for removing obstacles or being the obstacle? A reputation for finding the solution or passing the blame? The answers matter to creating a Champion's brand of trust. Trust is *the* game changer.

Take a Time Out. Imagine people had a nickname for you. What would it be? Ask others today for their honest feedback on your nickname. "Pretend that every single person you meet has a sign around his or her neck that says, 'Make me feel important.' Not only will you succeed in sales, you will succeed in life." Mary Kay Ash.

Everyone is your customer. Go the extra mile. Tell people what you can do, give them options. Telling people what you can't do is annoying and a trust buster.

Does your success criteria include helping others? Consider the concept that it is not how bright you shine, but how bright you help others shine. The Most Valuable Players are those who care, help others go further and leave a legacy that ripples into eternity for the good of humanity.

Nothing is confidential. Don’t talk about your manager, your colleagues, the customers. Zip it up. As for gossiping, don’t. In most cases, it is not your story to tell.

Talking to each other is much better than talking about each other.

Who needs your smile today? Probably 99.9% of the people you meet today need your smile. In inspiring others, by default you inspire yourself.

You are always receiving feedback. *Do people smile or grimace when you approach?* Begin noticing if people smile and walk towards you or run for cover when they see you. If they are running for cover, it's highly unlikely you'll reap the satisfaction and rewards of having a championship team.

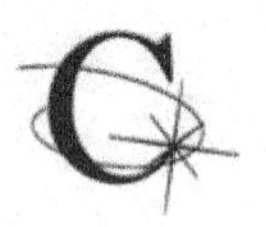

Receiving feedback builds your game. Ask for feedback if you are not receiving any. Listen to the feedback. Ask clarifying questions if needed in a non-defensive manner. Avoid making excuses or disqualifying the feedback given.

Everything communicates. ***There are no neutral actions.*** Everything you do either builds a sense of significance or destroys it. *Do people feel like heroes or zeroes in your presence?*

Women tend to underestimate their abilities. Take an inventory of your gifts and innate abilities. If you need to gain skill, do it. Understanding the financials is required. Speaking in front of people a must. "If you act enthusiastic, you'll be enthusiastic." A Dale Carnegie mantra that has served me well.

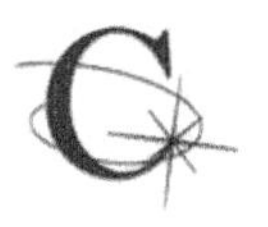

Many women have been taught that self-sacrifice makes for a "good" woman. Caring and pampering yourself actually make for a good *and* strong woman. Asking for and receiving help is a sign of strength, not weakness. Allow yourself the support. *Take care of you to take care of us.*

Disconnect from technology daily. Time does not have to be filled. Be still. Listen. "At the center of your being, you have the answer, you know who you are and you know what you want." Lao Tzu.

Women have the tendency to rescue and fight other individuals' battles. Allow others the gift of self-reliance. At times, protecting someone can do more harm than good. Ask yourself, "Is this my battle to take or is it part of someone else's growth and story?" It's situational rather you fight, coach, support or walk away.

Use discernment when choosing your battles. Some battles are simply distractions and not worth your energy. At times, you need to punt to win or refuse to engage. It's difficult to fight with someone who refuses to fight.

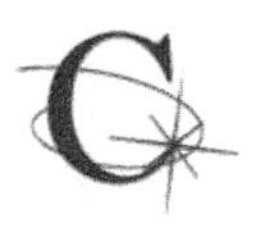

Follow your heart today. "Don't let your memories be bigger than your dreams." Stuntperson.

Should a man suggest you meet in his room, simply respond, "Considering today's climate, let's protect both our reputations and meet in the lobby." When a man asks you to get coffee, simply respond with a smile, "Let's go together so I can show you where it is for your future reference."

You are doing great. You're smiling more. You're owning your power more. You are getting wiser by considering your responses and the consequences more often. In fact, people are starting to notice your swagger!

Being bitter is giving a person or situation the energy you need for your game. They did you wrong. Got it. Stop making it an excuse for being distracted from making your vision a reality. Close the door on old hurts and offenses. Open doors to new possibilities.

You can be bitter or better. Never contaminate or limit your today with yesterday. "If you drink from a bottle marked 'poison', it is almost certain to disagree with you, sooner or later." Alice, *Alice in Wonderland*.

Not everyone is going to like you. Some individuals will come against you. Don't waste your energy on useless activities such as getting upset, being petty or retaliating. Instead keep being your best. The truth of the situation and your character will reveal itself. Adjust your jockstrap. You are being groomed with every tackle.

Every tackle is temporary. Only you can make the tackle a permanent injury.

If you have a male advocate, assume there might be rumors. Don't fuel the rumors with behaviors and actions that can be perceived as inappropriate. An example is dressing and acting like a femme fatale. Amazing women in provocative clothing are upset when they are not taken seriously. Seriously?

Just as perplexing a behavior is when a woman berates a man for opening her door. Opening doors regardless of gender is good manners, plain and simple.

Nothing is random. Everything has meaning. Every challenge is an opportunity to gain strength, experience and resiliency. A good visual for the bounce back factor is the blow-up punching clown. It bounces right back up regardless of the hit. ***You are more powerful than any hit.*** Stay centered and grounded in your truth and power.

It's okay to be happy. Give up the lies and depleting attitudes of well-meaning others and society. Choose life enhancing beliefs and thoughts. My favorites include: "Everything always works out for me." "I have zippo enemies, only teachers." "I'm not lost, just exploring." "They can't eat me." "Oops."

Take a Time Out. Close your eyes. Imagine your best friend is giving you a pep talk. Write the pep talk down. Now convert the pep talk into affirmations you can recite when feeling discouraged.

Only your own thoughts, emotions and actions can be controlled. If you are feeling wound up and stressed, it's time to focus on your breath and evaluate what you are thinking. *A change in perspective changes everything.* Choose happy.

Change your self-talk to retrain your mind. When triggered, immediately change your self-talk. Your manager is a major pain. "*Nice problem to have*, my boss is showing me what not to do." After a long day you get a flat tire. "*Well, that's amusing*, I have a flat tire. At least I have a car." Only you can make yourself miserable. Why be miserable?

People are complex. Where there are people there is drama. Believe people who tell you they are screwed up. Be cordial with everyone, not necessarily engaging. Cordial is common courtesy while engaging is active participation.

Being relaxed does not equal being lazy. Being relaxed is fuel to get your creative juices flowing and your stress down. What if you stopped trying to figure everything out and trusted the next step to appear? "Life simply took care of everything one step at a time." Louise Hay.

Never quit on you. There is always a dawn. The sun is always shining behind the clouds. Every day is filled with new mercy and grace. ***Always believe that something amazing is about to happen in your life.*** Reflect on when you felt the world was over. Then out of the blue, there was a connection, a fresh start. It happened before; it will happen again.

I am so proud of you! Give yourself a pat on the back and a cheer. How about some confetti? Go, you!

When you get the breath knocked out of you, take a time out. You grow with every tackle. *Your tormentors can be your best mentors.* You gain character, insights and humility for the next level of responsibility and authority. Dust yourself off and keep playing the game with new experience, determination and grace.

A mental fitness, strength building practice is taking 30 second gratitude breaks several times a day. As you feel the feeling of gratitude, put your hand over your heart to anchor the positive emotions. This practice is an energy fueler, a mood lifter and a stress buster to do what is yours to do refreshed and reenergized.

Encourage yourself. If you think you are at the end of your rope, cut the rope. Never insult or discredit yourself. Be your own cheering squad. You've got cheerleaders you don't even know about! ***You are loved more than you know.***

Everything is open to interpretation. Embrace it all. There is no punishment, only preparation to take you further than you thought possible. Every "bad" choice gets you closer to the right choice.

When you are exhausted or ready to throw in the towel, remember all of Heaven is cheering you on. Lean on their strength. Get some rest. Eat healthy. Visualize yourself pumping your arms in victory aka Rocky Balboa to "I Can Fly Now." You got what it takes. *You are that Champion.*

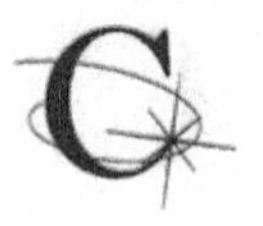

Life is messy and marvelous. Smile when you talk about yourself. Smile when you talk about the present. Smile when you talk about your future. Smile, it's contagious!

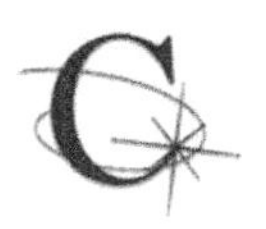

The drama is in your mind. Do not be swept away by your emotions. Everything is not a threat or personal attack. When triggered: Breathe. Smile. Repeat. Try new responses. "That's an interesting perspective." "Tell me more." "Help me understand what is behind that comment."

There is always a choice. There is always an option. Choose wisely.

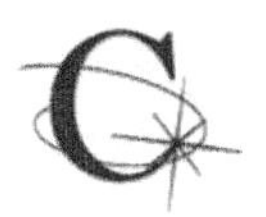

Assume good intent until proven otherwise. If proven otherwise, be cautious in your future dealings with that person. Be 100% discerning. A few people lie like breathing. Be definitive in setting your boundaries and expectations. Immediately call out a bad play. Do more follow-up with that person to ensure your reputation stays intact.

When you notice a man speaking to your boobs, consider stating, "They don't talk." When a man makes a lewd remark, consider responding with, "Why would you think I'd want to know that?"

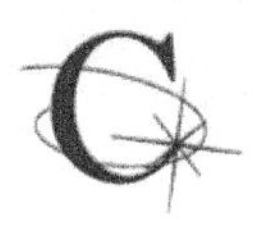

Some men have the tendency to grab their crotches in front of women. If you are becoming uncomfortable, you might ask with a concerned look, "Have you've seen a doctor for that itch?" "Perhaps one has to become very old before one learns to be amused rather than offended." Pearl S. Buck.

To be annoyed and to keep score when you haven't shared your unwritten ground rules and expectations is unfair and cr-aaa-zy. Actually, keeping score is cr-aaa-zy. Do what is yours to do without expecting kudos or thanks. *Do it for you.*

Identify 2 emotions you want to feel during the day. Use these emotions as your guide as you move through the day. For example, you might want to feel compassion for yourself and others or feeling faith over fear. You can intentionally make it your best day ever. ***You are that powerful.***

An inconvenience and a problem are *very* different. An inconvenience is a molehill. A problem is a mountain to be scaled. Stop catastrophizing. Make your life easier by seeing molehills for what they are, not what you imagine. *Change your pattern of thinking and everything changes.*

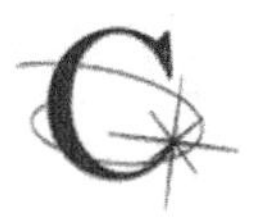

Worry is suffering twice. "I have been through some terrible things in my life, some of which actually happened." Mark Twain.

Guard your thoughts, choose the good ones.
You are mastering the game!

Differing realities create tension and conflict. Conflict does not equate with rejection. Override your emotions. Ask more questions to understand the person's perspective, pain point and priorities. Listen intently with an open mind. Stay in the conversation regardless of how uncomfortable. Solve the pain, be the Champion.

Men, in general, take conflict and comments in stride as part of the game. Women tend to ruminate and take it personally. It's never personal even though it feels personal. If you feel it is, gain clarity one-on-one with the person once the emotional edge is off. Confrontation conversations go much better when you are energy neutral.

Confront and deal with issues immediately. Never assume they will go away. If you do not address the problem, you become part of the problem. *If you are having a lot of issues and conflict in your life, could it be you?*

People pleasing and being an approval junkie are not generally patterning for men. They just take the perceived hit, adjust their jockstrap and keep playing. Smart play.

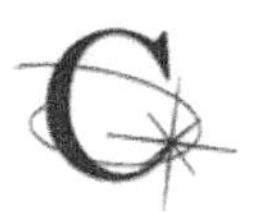

Men have the tendency to take credit for their team's success. Women tend to give credit to the team. You can have the best of both worlds. The next time your team has a success, try saying something like, "Leading the team to success is exciting. We're building our future capacity together."

Change is inevitable and constant. Thus the game changes - new players, new rules, new managers. You can get depressed, collapse into despair and play the victim. You can fight the change, get beat up and at best survive. Or you can choose to grow with the change by embracing and adapting to it.

Champions expand through their fears to adapt and thrive. Say "*yes, I can*" to moving past your comfort zone. Thriving is the choice of champions. You are *that* Champion!

Imagine there was a word that describes change for you. What would it be? *Your mental attitude impacts your adaptability.* Being adaptable and resilient to curve balls strengthens your game. Resiliency is a deal maker or breaker for all genders. You are far more resilient than you realize.

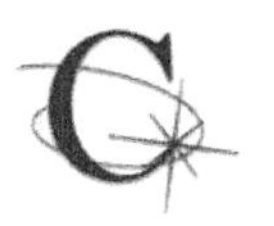

If you find yourself questioning why something is happening or has happened, remember *there are no wasted experiences.* "Please help me see everything as a blessing God." "It is a blessing."

You are not ordinary. You are exceptional! You were made on purpose for a purpose only you can fulfill! You are meant for greatness and winning the game at work and in life.

Feeling stressed and overwhelmed? Take a shake break. Shaking your body while smiling releases tension and stress. Other activities that help reduce stress include: Go for a short walk. Take 5 minutes to consciously breathe - "Breathing in. Breathing out." Take 3 minutes to visualize your bright future or think of a person or pet that instantly brings a smile to your heart.

Do you need to be right at all costs? What's wrong with being wrong? Nothing! No one has all the right answers.

Redefine failure. There is none except giving up on yourself.

Remember your last networking event. Whose business card did you keep? The person looking over your shoulder constantly for the next person or the person who gave you their undivided attention? Be fully present to make a positive impression. "I see you." Avatar.

Women have been taught getting angry is bad and unladylike. Anger is normal and your coach. It is a sign something is off. Question the anger. Identify what is at the root of the anger. Then decide the best course of action.

Thoughts drive your actions. Every action creates a reaction that impacts your destiny. There are no neutral actions.

Being personable and likable are good. Being both is *not* the same as being a doormat or contortionist. "No" is a complete sentence. *You are always setting the standards for the way people treat you.*

Make the best of where you are now. Delete the words "can't" and "impossible" from your vocabulary. Exchange "have to" for "get to." You are where you are for a reason. A change in wording can change your perspective and attitude. An optimistic, can-do attitude scores big.

Bullies come in all colors, ages and genders. Your options include avoiding the person if you can, minimizing your interactions or walking away. Do not engage, it is a waste of energy. *If you see a punch coming, DUCK.* Just because you know you can take a punch doesn't mean you need to. When appropriate, notify the correct person of the bullying.

Being a bully, defiant and belligerent doesn't gain respect for any gender.

Never apologize for being a badass with a smile and having unshakeable confidence. It's perfectly okay to flex your muscles when necessary. Being strong and "a lot of woman" is a good thing. Know your audience to know when to throttle back your persona to give people breathing room.

Striving for excellence gets results and garners a solid reputation. Striving for perfection causes frustration for you and for others. Give up performance issues. Give up jumping through hoops. Give up struggle and strain. Perseverance is a very good thing. Stubbornness, not so much.

True champions are humble, not arrogant. Humility and a calm certainty are brand builders. Invisibility though? "Yes" to being humble. "No" to being invisible.

Own your life. Own your choices. Own your consequences. Own your definition of success to own your swagger and authenticity.

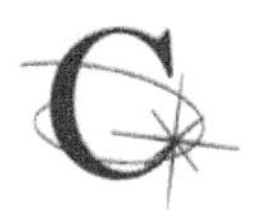

Invest in yourself. Invest in your personal development. Invest in your wardrobe. Invest in your brand. Invest in you to achieve your goals, dreams and heart's desires. "We are the ones we've been waiting for." Oraibi Elders.

Emotions are signposts. *You are not your emotions.* Begin monitoring and questioning your emotions. Is this emotion appropriate for the situation? Consider smiling internally next time you are offended by a comment or a perceived slight. Respond intentionally versus reacting emotionally.

If you are unhappy, ask yourself: "Is there a good reason for my unhappiness or is this a pattern?" If a good reason, feel the emotions then let them dissolve to create a solution. If unhappiness is a pattern, allow yourself to be happy. "Don't take life too seriously. You'll never get out of it alive." Señor Frog T-Shirt.

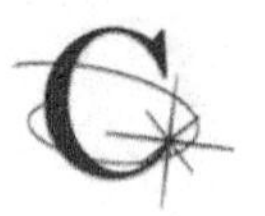

It is virtually impossible to be upset and grateful at the same time. Choose gratitude for the "upsetting" coaching moment. You are being prepared for the next play.

You know what is good for you. Listen and use your body's wisdom. When you enter a person's presence, do you feel relaxed or do you tense up? Do you feel uplifted or do you feel on guard? The same body wisdom applies with *all* people and in *all* situations.

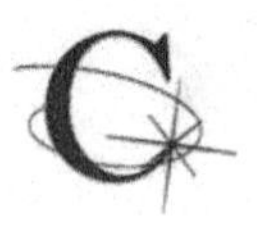

Life is madly in love with you. Everything happens for you, not to you. Perceived difficulties and obstacles are vital strength training. Detours are redirects to get you where you need to be. Everything is an advantage. "It's not the load that breaks you. It's the way you carry it." Lena Horn.

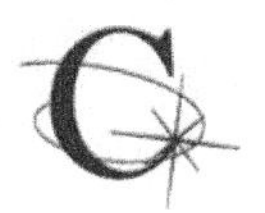

A shift in perspective changes everything! "One moment the world is as it is. The next, it is something entirely different. Something it has never been before." Anne Rice.

Surround yourself with people who are uplifting, who are advocates, who model what you want and who will up your game. Spend more time with people who make you smile, giggle and laugh.

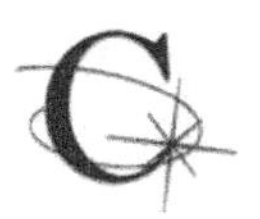

Minimize spending time with people who are always finding fault with life and with you. Avoid people who give you emotional hangovers. Sometimes you just need to walk away - you needn't announce it.

Take a Time Out. Reflect on your 5 closest relationships. Write their names, then ask yourself these questions: "Does this relationship give me energy and peace or create drama and unrest? Does this relationship support my dreams or dismiss them? Does this relationship build my brand or diminish it?" Do any of your relationships need updating?

You can't control what comes your way. You can control your response. *Rule your emotions instead of them ruling you.* Why would you let someone steal your energy, your power and your joy? "You can often change your circumstances by changing your attitude." Eleanor Roosevelt.

There are no failures, only learnings. Self-correction is amazing. Self-condemnation is overkill. There are no brownie points for suffering. Progress, not perfection. "Though I walk through the valley of death, I do not have to build a home there." Louise Hay.

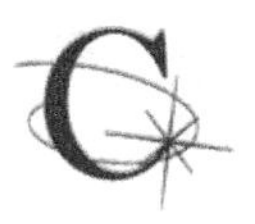

Being happy with yourself creates inside out confidence, power and enthusiasm. Practice choosing life-affirming, enriching and happy thoughts until they become your new norm. Being happy is an inspiration to others and builds a bigger team. The bigger your team, the better.

Exaggerate your good. Give yourself kudos and celebrate your many gifts, your good choices and your successes. Keep a running list of every single success. There's always something to celebrate. Some days just showing up can be a huge win.

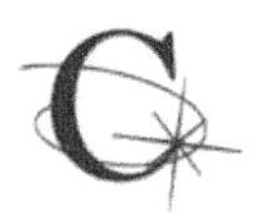

Meetings are important. Arrive early to meetings to ensure a seat at the table. Be strategic where you sit. Be prepared. Be the first to smile. Give a solid handshake. Be engaged. Take notes by hand so not to be perceived as texting. Sit up straight, shoulders relaxed. Listen intently. Look people in the eye. Contribute.

Men tend to get to the point and be more concise in their communications. Time is money. Your time is priceless. Be concise, straight forward and do not dance around the issue. As a point of reference, men tend not to give external signs or verbal clues that they are listening. Don't expect validation.

When you attend a meeting with 100% males, adjust your jockstrap – they can't eat you. If during the meeting you are consistently being spoken over, breathe and stand up. Smile and state your message concisely. Yes, it takes courage. Yes, it works.

If you are in a meeting or on a call, and someone asks you something you don't know reply with, "I'll find out and get back to you." There is no reason to explain why you don't know. Never make up an answer.

Learning keeps you mentally strong, sustains your relevancy and ups your brand at work and in life.

Our nature as women is to collaborate and be a team player. Good for business. Do take notice, however, when your good spirit of collaboration is being taken advantage. Then take action to reset the rules of the game.

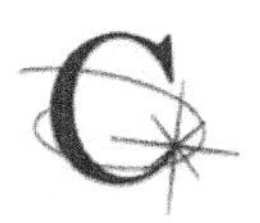

Establishing boundaries and ground rules for interactions is a sound play. Speak up for yourself at the first sign of feeling ill at ease or feeling disrespected. No need to be defensive or defiant. Breathe. Clearly state your boundary and expectation for moving forward.

Men, in general, place a higher value on problem solving and gaining results. Women, in general, tend to place a higher value on the relationships. In the workplace, solutions and results get rewarded. Be a champion in the workplace by attaining better solutions and results through relationships of trust.

Keep your sense of humor to keep your sanity and the game interesting and fun. "You grow up the day you have the real first laugh at yourself." Ethel Barrymore.

Some women tend to go for sainthood. If you choose to go for sainthood, good for you. Please keep it to yourself. Being a martyr is not the same as sainthood. Martyrs are exasperating to those around them.

Falling down and getting back up is part of the game. Adverse conditions are temporary and steppingstones to opportunities. In the back of your mind, remind yourself, "I've already survived 100% of my worst days. I'm still standing."

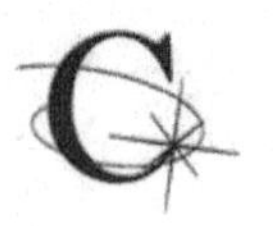

When at a loss or lost, *choose to do the next right thing.* It will work out. You are at the right place at the right time. Relax. Breathe. Smile. "The greater part of happiness or misery depends on our disposition, not our circumstances." Martha Washington.

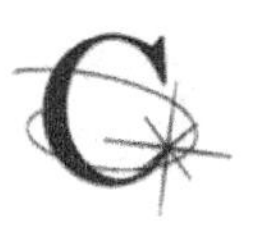

You must get past your need to be liked by everyone. Stop holding on when you know it is time to let go. If you must hold on, what is your perceived payoff? Is being liked worth squandering your power or losing your soul and spirit?

Celebrate all relationships – past, present and future. All relationships taught you something. Even if the "something" is learning how to forgive. As you forgive others, you are forgiving yourself. Strange, but true. Often, we are actually mad at ourselves for allowing the betrayal, the rude behavior or whatever.

Forgiveness is not condoning the behavior. Forgiveness is setting you free from toxic emotions and the past.

Forgive yourself for all the ways you feel or think you have let yourself and others down. Now is your moment of power to make amends and course correct. Saying "Oops!" is certainly better than beating yourself up ad nauseum. Apologize if warranted and move on with grace.

"Good-bye, Past. Thank you for the learnings. Hello, Future! I'm ready to live life fully today!" Self-righteousness keeps us stuck in the past and poisons today with yesterday. And more than likely, the person has already moved on.

Everything is a coaching moment. Everyone is on your team for greatness – no exceptions. Be coachable and a life-long learner.

Breakdowns lead to breakthroughs. No event, circumstance or person can extinguish your light permanently. Only you can. Be prepared by the past, not defined by it. *No one holds you hostage but you.* "Optimism is the faith that leads to achievement. Nothing can be done without faith and optimism." Helen Keller.

Live consciously. Be present and mindful to live in the now. Plan for the future, do not live there. ***Now is your moment.*** You can change the course of your life with a change in thought or belief. *You have the power!*

Redirect. Reframe. It's only a thought and thoughts can be changed. You have the power to reclaim your power in every moment. Triggers are simply friends in disguise to uncover your limiting constructs. Observe and quiz your emotions. They are your personal strength trainer. Situations and people don't control your emotions, you do.

Be more successful by replacing expectations with preferences. Replacing judgment with discernment and mercy. Replacing bitterness with compassion. Everyone is doing the best they know how in any given situation. "If you are rubbed by every rub, how will you be polished?" Rumi.

Stop engaging with negative, toxic people. If the toxic person is your manager, breathe. Manage your exposure to him/her. Keep the conversations cordial, short and about how you can contribute to their success. Don't poke the bear.

Stop all blame, guilt and self-sabotage regardless of the perceived sin. The original meaning of sin was "missing the target." Every Champion misses the target on the way to championships.

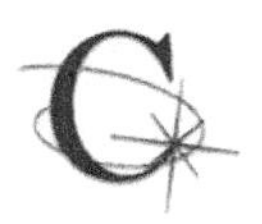

What obstacles? They are all opportunities. *Change the language and you change the energy.* "To reach something good it is useful to have gone astray and thus acquire experience." St. Teresa of Avila.

A change in pace changes everything. Take a dance break to get your fun and fabulous back. Some great songs include: Abba's "Dancing Queen," Taylor Swift's "Shake It Off," Selena Gomez's "Who Says," Katy Perry's "Roar" and "Firework," "This Is Me" from *The Greatest Showman*, "I Hope You Dance" by Lee Ann Womack and "Celebrate!" by Kool and The Gang.

Take a Time Out. Have some fun. Create your own Championship playlist. Make sure it gives you hope, pumps you up, flexes your muscles and gets you excited for the big game.

Every word you speak matters. Every thought you think matters. Every emotion you feel matters. Every action you take matters. ***You matter.***

Everything you do either adds to your credibility or destroys it. Everything you do either builds the self-esteem of others or destroys it. Everything you do either creates inclusion or creates isolation. Choose like the victorious Champion that you are.

Choose to live today, not someday. *Choose deliberately to be for yourself* to up your game and set the world on fire as only you can.

Hello, Champion! *Change your thoughts, change your world, change the world.* Your future is so bright you are going to need sunglasses. "Be who God meant you to be, and you will set the world on fire." St. Catherine of Siena

ABOUT YOUR COACH

Ellen Castro, Chief Energizing Officer, is a trusted executive coach, an award-winning, best-selling author, a globally recognized business and leadership consultant and impactful speaker. She has been selected Global Female Executive Coach of the Year for 2019 and 2020 by Acquisition International. Ellen is your catalyst for growth and success on all levels. With caring candor, she brings light to beliefs and behaviors blocking your advancement. Her proven framework for establishing relationships of trust makes a tangible lasting impact on her clients' success. Ellen has touched millions via life changing keynotes and media appearances. Her books, *Spirited Leadership: 52 Ways to Build Trust* and *Happy in Spite of People* inspire change by providing pragmatic tools and insights on how to gain credibility, earn followership and attain authentic self-confidence.

After earning a BBA and MBA from Southern Methodist University, Ellen joined Exxon where she led a $90M profit center of 500 employees. She became the highest-ranking female in Marketing, earning 6 promotions in 11 years. She then decided to reinvent herself. Upon completing her MEd at Harvard University, Ellen directed the merger/acquisition process for a national healthcare alliance that grew from 1,000 to 5,000 employees prior to becoming an entrepreneur in 1991. She has served on the faculty of SMU's Edwin L. Cox Business Leadership Center and taught the inaugural *Latinas and Leadership* class at the University of North Texas.

Is this me?! *Who would have guessed my mess would become my miracle. And I want to be yours! You are my why.*

Perhaps sharing my story will give you hope, strength and confidence to stay in the game. You are far greater than anything you encounter. My childhood was a war zone. My earliest memories of my Latina mom are her telling me she had tried to abort me and failed. She delighted in saying God didn't even want me. Life with her was anything but easy. She was bi-polar and committed suicide while I was attending college.

As for my dad, he was a machismo raging alcoholic. He told me, "Thank God you are smart, no man could ever love you." He quit school in the sixth-grade to provide food and shelter for his mom and himself. When he was 17, his mom committed suicide. He enlisted in the military. Upon return from the Army, he met his first cousin – my mom – and they were married 2 weeks later. He wanted to give her the good life so he took the only job he could get delivering flowers. He worked like a dog, moved up and became a very successful florist and businessman. When I was just 6 years old, I started working at his flower shop. He said I needed to learn how to support myself – there would be no Prince for me. Elpidio Brambilla Castro showed me how to play the game in a white world. He changed his name to E.B. because he was sure his clients couldn't pronounce Elpidio, plus it was "too Mexican." E.B. passed me his drive and sound business mind.

To add to my childhood trauma, I was repeatedly sexually abused by a relative. The devastation on my psyche is inexpressible. I now realize that all of these experiences were preparation to become the person I am today. Needing to prove my worth as a person, woman and Mexican spurred me on to excel at school. Wanting to find acceptance led to extracurricular activities that served me well. *Most importantly, at an early age I knew my heart's desire. My purpose was to help others feel their worth and see their greatness.*

Fast forward to Exxon in the 1970s as a bright MBA Latina in the oil and gas industry. I worked 24/7, guzzled vodka and munched on anti-depressants to numb the pain while scrambling up the corporate ladder amidst the racial slurs, groping and daily harassment. I defined success by position and promotion regardless of the costs to my soul. As mentioned in the Preface, my seventh promotion was blocked by my vice-president. I asked, "Why?" He simply stated, "I don't like you." The invisible glass ceiling I had attempted to break, *finally* broke me.

Thank heaven for grace. A few months later, an out of the blue divine connection resulted in me finding myself attending Harvard in 1986. One of my greatest epiphanies from the coursework was learning infants are born with only 2 fears, the rest are mind-made. *What is mind-made can be changed.* With weekly counseling, I began changing my perception of myself and my perspective of the world. The personal growth and adventure are ongoing – I'm still breathing. Today I choose self-awareness, prayer and happiness over guzzling vodka, munching on antidepressants and pain. I am humbled by God's countless miracles and for doing what I thought was impossible – turning ashes into beauty.

In 2008, Charlie, a former Exxon colleague emailed, "The world would not be a better place for you to have broken through the glass ceiling." He was right. *Because I lost my soul, I can show you how not to lose your soul and how you can succeed beyond your wildest imagination in a man's world.*

We all have stories. We are not our stories. We can overcome anything by changing our mindset and narrative. We, as women and people who have been marginalized, need to break through the deeply engrained societal patterns and cultural myths. I "know our place." It is in the boardroom as colleagues and thought partners, not in the shadows, relegated to subservient, dismissive roles. *I also know the best way to break the societal myths is through example.* We change the game from the inside. This raw uncensored playbook shows you how.

Research indicates that the number one factor keeping women from rising up the corporate ladder is *lack of self-confidence*. Women, it is time to own our energy and power. It is time to be excited that we are strong instead of being secretly ashamed of our strength. Now is our time to call out the nonsense with a smile, including the nonsense in our minds.

Your life has meaning. You are far more powerful and resilient than you know. You are loved more than you know. You are the game changer. Adjust your jockstrap. You have what it takes. *With faith and better choices, choose to be Champion you are created to be. Dare to be your most authentic and powerful self!* I'm with you in spirit every step of the way, cheering you on. Godspeed!

If you'd like to work directly with me as your Coach, please reach out by emailing Ellen@EllenCastro.com. We can discuss your customized game plan to win at work and in life. For additional information, you can go to https://ellencastro.com/coaching/.

Made in the USA
Middletown, DE
26 May 2021

40421919R00139